All About Plants

All About

Seeds

Claire Throp

Heinemann
LIBRARY

Chicago, Illinois

Edited by Claire Throp and Brynn Baker
Designed by Peggie Carley
Picture research by Ruth Blair
Production by Victoria Fitzgerald
Originated by Capstone Global Library Ltd
Printed and bound in China by RR Donnelley Asia

18 17 16 15 14
10 9 8 7 6 5 4 3 2 1

Library of Congress Cataloging-in-Publication Data
is on file with the Library of Congress.

ISBN 978-1-4846-0509-7 (hardcover)

ISBN 978-1-4846-0515-8 (ebook PDF)

Acknowledgments
We would like to thank the following for
permission to reproduce photographs:
Alamy: Dirk v. Mallinckrodt, 18, 23 (middle);
Getty Images: S.J. Krasemann, 19; Shutterstock:
2009fotofriends, 4, AlessandroZocc, back cover,
13, Charles Brutlag, 21, 23 (bottom), Daleen
Loest, 16, Elenadesign, 10, Filipe B. Varela, 5, Jose
Ignacio Soto, 22, Mazzzur, 8, 23 (top), Michal
Zduniak, 15, Nikita Tiunov, 17, Photoexpert, 9,
Pressmaster, 20, Rimantas Abromas, 7, Spiber, 6,
sunsetman, 11, Thomas Klee, 12, Vitaly Ilyasov, 14;
Superstock: Tips Images/Maurizio Polverelli, cover

We would like to thank Michael Bright for his
invaluable help in the preparation of this book.

Every effort has been made to contact copyright
holders of material reproduced in this book.
Any omissions will be rectified in subsequent
printings if notice is given to the publisher.

Contents

What Are Plants?

Plants are living things.

flower

stem

leaf

root

seed

Plants have
many parts.

What Do Plants Need to Grow?

Plants need sunlight and air to grow.

Plants need water to grow.

What Are Seeds?

seed

A seed is one part of a plant.
Flowers make seeds.

New plants grow from seeds.

Different Seeds

seed

Some plants have lots
of small seeds.

seed

Some plants have big seeds.

Some seeds are round.

Some seeds have wings.

Spreading Seeds

Some birds eat seeds.

These birds drop seeds
in new places.

The wind blows some seeds
through the air.

The seeds land far away from
the old plant.

Some seeds burst out of **pods**.

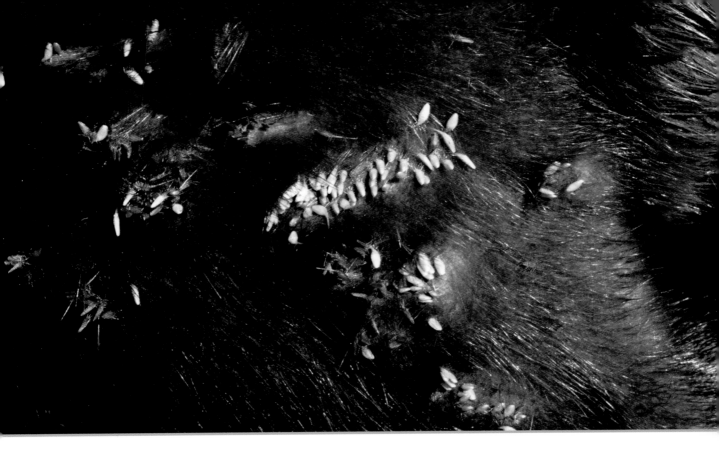

Some seeds hook onto animals' fur.
Animals carry seeds to new places.

How Seeds Grow

Seeds usually grow in the ground.

seed

root

They grow **roots**.

Plants Need Seeds

Seeds grow into new plants.
The new plants make new seeds.

Picture Glossary

 **flower** part of a plant that blossoms and makes new seeds

 **pod** part of some plants in which seeds grow safely inside

 **root** part of a plant used to absorb water from the ground

Index

Notes for Parents and Teachers

Before reading

Find out how much children know about seeds. Make sure they understand that most plants grow from seeds and that most seeds grow in the ground.

After reading

- Gather a selection of seeds for children to investigate. Provide magnifying glasses for children to use to examine the seeds. Have children group the seeds by size, shape, and/or color.

- Draw simple pictures of the sequence of plant growth on separate cards. For example, seed in the ground, roots growing, shoot growing, stem forming, leaves appearing, flowers blossoming. Make copies of each card. Divide the class into groups. Children can work together to put the cards in the correct order.

- Provide a small pot, soil, and seed to individual, pairs, or small groups. Demonstrate how to plant and care for the seeds. Allow time for children to observe plant growth.